DIVORCE
AND YOUR FAMILY™

UNDERSTANDING YOUR PARENTS' DIVORCE

BECKY LENARKI AND FLORENCE CALHOUN

ROSEN
PUBLISHING®
New York

Published in 2017 by The Rosen Publishing Group, Inc.
29 East 21st Street, New York, NY 10010

First Edition

Library of Congress Cataloging-in-Publication Data

Names: Lenarki, Becky, author. | Calhoun, Florence, author.
Title: Understanding your parents' divorce / Becky Lenarki and Florence Calhoun.

Description: First edition. | New York : Rosen Publishing, 2017. | Series:
 Divorce and your family | Includes bibliographical references and index.
Identifiers: LCCN 2015044298 | ISBN 9781508171270 (library bound)
Subjects: LCSH: Children of divorced parents—Juvenile literature. |
Divorce—Juvenile literature.

Classification: LCC HQ777.5 .L45 2016 | DDC 306.89--dc23
LC record available at http://lccn.loc.gov/2015044298

Manufactured in China

CONTENTS

INTRODUCTION

If you think about your future, you probably assume that eventually—not any time soon!—you will get married and have a family of your own. This is how our society was organized when the first colonists settled in America, and it remains largely the same today.

Almost no one predicts that they will be divorced in their lifetime. It's just not something that people wish for themselves. It would be hard to imagine the circumstances under which divorce was one of someone's life goals.

Marriage is what follows after the joy and excitement of a wedding. As any married couple will tell you, marriage is a lot of work and is not something to be taken lightly. There are ups and downs, highs and lows, good times and bad. Many people believe that because they have committed to spending a lifetime with their spouse, they must figure out how to weather any storms that come up over their lifetime, no matter what.

But for some people, the pain of an unhappy marriage isn't worth enduring for the rest of their lives. They would tell you that it's better to admit that the marriage ran its course and move on

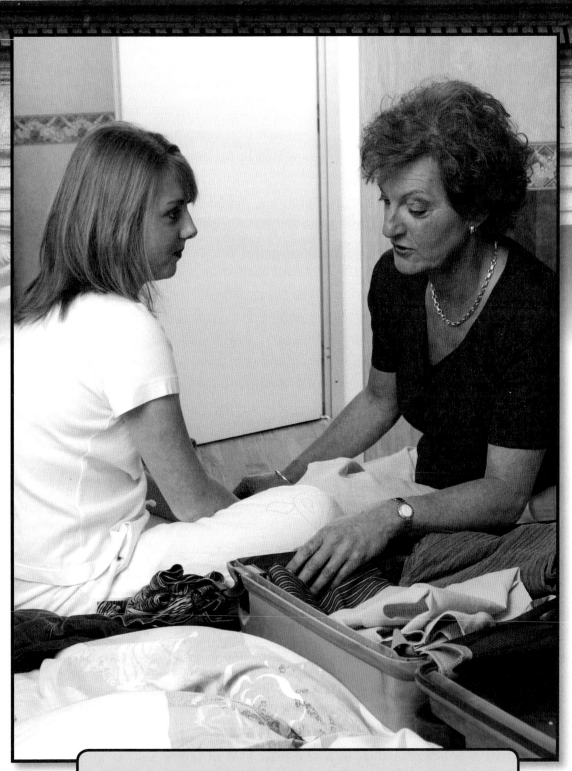

When your parents tell you they're getting a divorce, all kinds of feelings will rush into your head. You may be so busy thinking about how your life will change that you don't think about what your parents are going through.

in search of the next step. Perhaps there are serious issues in the marriage, like substance abuse or domestic violence, that break a marriage beyond repair. Or perhaps one partner realized he or she doesn't love the other and wants to be free to spend his or her life with someone else.

Regardless of the circumstances, divorce happens. And it happens fairly often. Statistics vary, but according to the Centers for Disease Control and Prevention, approximately 36 percent of marriages in the United States end in divorce. Chances are you know at least one person whose parents are divorced.

But what if that person is you? Have your parents recently told you they are divorcing? Are you having trouble making sense of it, even after the shock has worn off? Whether your parents always seemed happy together or whether they fought all the time, it's never easy to see them split up. It's a confusing time for everyone.

No doubt you will experience a world of changes. One of your parents will no longer live with you. You may stay with him or her on weekends or whenever your parents agree. You might have to move to a different house or apartment. You might even have to change schools. Your schedule will change, and holidays will be completely different. You might even have to cope with a stepparent and stepsiblings if your parents eventually marry other people.

So how can your parents, who supposedly love you, do this to you? Why would they put you through all this, when growing up is hard enough even under the best of circumstances?

The answer is, your parents aren't doing it to you. Even though their divorce affects you in many ways, it is the breakup of their marriage. They will no longer be spouses, but they will not stop being your parents.

This point may seem obvious, but it's very important to understand. It means that to help yourself through the pain of your parents' divorce, you must first step back and consider what they're going through. Their marriage, which they thought would last forever, has ended, and that brings on more sadness and anger than you can imagine.

Once you realize your parents are just as upset as you are, you can begin to move forward. Knowing that they are going through a terrible time along with you gives you the opportunity to share your feelings and your fears, and to chart your new territory together. No one wants to go through a divorce, but if you find yourself in this situation, it doesn't have to be the end of the world.

CHAPTER ONE

SO YOUR PARENTS ARE GETTING A DIVORCE

Everyone has been there, heard about it, or seen it in a movie: that fateful day when the parents sit the family down for a serious talk. They tell the kids that no matter how hard they tried, they can no longer be together as a couple. It's not the kids' fault. And whatever happens, they love them very much and will not stop being their parents.

It doesn't always happen this way, of course. Every talk is different. Some kids don't even get a talk. But chances are, if you do find yourself listening to this kind of talk, your life is about to change forever.

Jacob's parents had been fighting a lot. Even his little brother, Max, had picked up on the bitterness and hostility around the house. It might have started when their father lost his job last year. Money was tight, and arguments between their parents increased to the point where they couldn't be in the same room without yelling at each other.

Everyone reacts differently to the news that their parents are splitting up. Some kids are surprised, while others are relieved. Some are angry, while others are sad. Listen to what your parents say and tell them how you feel.

Jacob couldn't take it anymore. He spent as much time as possible at school or with his friends. He didn't think his parents even noticed. One night he came home and found that his mother was gone. Jacob's father said she'd left that morning to drive out to Jacob's grandparents' five states away. Jacob couldn't believe his mother didn't want to take him and Max, or even wait around to say good-bye.

The Need for a Stable Home

Though Jacob was disappointed by his parents' decision, he was not totally surprised. He was somewhat prepared. At least he had known that his parents were not happy. Often teens will see that their parents are not getting along, but they might hold on to the hope that they will work out their differences. Jacob obviously did not like the fighting between them and was hurt by the instability and uncertainty of their lives, but he did not like the thought of the breakup either.

You might react to your situation in one way, but someone else might react in quite another. As the fighting and hostility between Jacob's parents grew, so did his sense of discontentment with the family's situation. A home should be a place of shelter, love, and security. These qualities were not available to Jacob. The lack of these essential ingredients for a stable home life affected the entire household.

It is extremely difficult for children to witness long-term fighting and hostility between parents, the two people on whom children rely to provide their most basic needs. Teenagers are likely to be going through tremendous physiological, social, and emotional changes independent of whatever their parents are experiencing. Teens are involved in the business of growing up, engaging in the normal and natural changes of this stage of their development. Males and females have passed through puberty and are beginning to establish themselves socially.

For most teens, how their peers view them is very important. They are finding their own identity while exploring relationships with the opposite sex. This can be very complicated and made even more difficult when they are simultaneously being confronted with the breakup of their family. It seems to say that even the deepest romantic relationships are impermanent, hurtful, and even destructive.

During this difficult period, most teens experience a number

When your parents argue, it can be especially upsetting if you're a teen. This is a stage in your life when you are exploring relationships with the opposite sex. Experiencing disharmony at home can dampen your hopes.

of conflicting thoughts and feelings. When your parents argue, you want to put as much distance between you as you possibly can. You might wonder why you sometimes want to scream and run out of the house. You might wonder why you feel as though you want to take charge of your own life. You might feel as though you want to take over the leadership role from your parents. In one sense, you might feel more grown up than they are because your parents, in your eyes, are no longer acting reasonably.

Jacob chose to distance himself by finding a family away from home. This family away from home was a substitute, or surrogate, for his real family. He found friends that would accept him and make him feel that he belonged. He began to stay out late at night, not letting his parents know where he was going or when he would return. He wanted to be independent and run his own life. Jacob was suffering, but he did not know why or how to effectively deal with his pain. For a long time he had suffered in silence when his parents argued. The months and years of witnessing hostility between his parents had hardened him; yet, they did not erase his yearning for closeness and belonging.

It is normal for teens to be somewhat preoccupied with their own feelings and needs. The normal physiological, social, and emotional changes that teens undergo during these years require the support and wisdom of parents if healthy development is to occur. When parents are distracted by their own problems, they may find it difficult to provide such support. For teens, this can cause conflicting feelings and changes (sometimes dramatic changes) in behavior, which is called acting out.

Mya, age sixteen, a junior in high school, was totally surprised when her parents told her they were getting a divorce. Mya and her younger sister, Brielle, age thirteen, were both happy, popular girls. Mya played on the girls' basketball team and was very involved in her church. She worked extremely hard to earn decent grades in school. Brielle was close to her older sister and tried to follow her example. Both were close to their parents, whom they believed loved each other deeply. Neither child had any idea that the marriage was in trouble. Obviously their parents had their differences, as Mya found out, but they were able to keep from arguing in front of their children.

Their parents broke the news to the girls one evening after dinner. The girls' dad revealed that he wanted a change and that he would be moving out of the house. He had already told Mya's mom that he had fallen in love with the woman with whom he had been having an affair for the past few months. Both parents explained the hopelessness of their marriage. They announced that the divorce was certain.

When You're Caught Off Guard

In contrast to Jacob's situation, the decision to separate can happen quite suddenly in some families, leaving the children totally unprepared and causing shock and dismay. When divorce in their family happens suddenly, teens naturally wonder what will happen to them and whether their lives will ever be normal again.

The fear of the unknown is common to all humans. All of us fear change, and divorce brings many changes. When news of a divorce arrives as a sudden announcement, it can be a profound shock to your emotions and may produce an immediate feeling of uncertainty and a lack of confidence and hope for the future.

The fear of change gripped Mya so tightly that she began to fall apart in many ways. She found herself unwilling or unable to talk to either of her parents or confide in anyone at school. Her situation was so overwhelming to her that she found it difficult to study or take part in any of her normal activities. She lost interest in the things that had been most important to her before

Divorce brings change, and some people are not able to cope with change. Rather than try to adapt, some teens give up control and completely withdraw into themselves.

and that had seemed such a natural part of her personality. Her grades dropped, and she no longer associated with her friends. Sadness, fear, and loneliness seemed to take over completely.

Although Jacob was somewhat prepared for his parents' separation and Brielle and Mya were not, these teens had a couple of important things in common. They were both deeply affected by what was happening in their families, and their responses were completely natural and understandable under the circumstances. This is not the same thing as saying that they were the only possible responses or that all the pain these teens experienced was absolutely inevitable.

CHAPTER TWO

THE MANY EMOTIONS OF DIVORCE

The end of a marriage is a very painful time. Some people refer to divorce as a death because it is the death of a marriage. As with any loss, those reacting to it experience a series of complex emotions and behaviors. Some psychologists refer to these as the stages of grief, and depending on the model, most agree that the process of achieving acceptance involves five or seven distinct emotions. Children whose parents are divorcing often work through the stages of grief, which roughly follow the route outlined below. Not everyone experiences the emotions in this order, and some people repeat one or more stages.

Stage 1: Denial

When you first realize that your parents are going to separate or divorce, your immediate response might be disbelief. You might not want to believe it, or you might wish that it would not happen. You might go around telling yourself that you do not really care, that it does not matter one way or the other, or that you are not going to show anyone how much it hurts. These responses can be positive or negative, depending on such factors as their

Denial is an early stage of the grieving process. During this period, you may not want to address your feelings or even admit that anything is wrong at all. Denial is a natural stage, but you need to work through it.

duration and extremity—that is, how long these feelings last, how intense they are, and how you act them out. Denial is a way of easing the pain that you are feeling. Denial is our way of protecting ourselves from what we believe will be a dreadful experience. To a certain extent this works. However, when denial stops you from reaching any of the other stages, even more serious problems can result.

Brielle, Mya's sister, was in denial about her parents' divorce. While Mya responded with withdrawal and depression, Brielle continued to go on with her activities as before. It appeared as though she was OK. If anyone asked how she was doing, Brielle's answer was always the same: "Fine." While her sister struggled, Brielle dug deeper into her school activities than she ever had before. Pretending, for her own protection, that everything was the same, Brielle became compulsive about her activities and her school work. She minimized, or made light of, her feelings of loss.

Many people regard carrying on in the face of a profound loss, as if nothing has happened, to be brave or courageous. In many ways it is or can be. However, when such behavior prevents you from accessing all your feelings about the loss, even greater long-term problems can result.

Stage 2: Anger

When you experience an emotional shock, anger is a common response. You may wonder why your parents got married in the first place. You may get mad because you feel like a victim. Victims feel helpless because bad things have happened to them that they did not cause and that they cannot remedy. Everyone likes to feel that they have control over their life. You may be angry because you know that your life will change, and in the beginning stages of the divorce, you may not be sure what this change will mean in your life. The following are typical ways that teens express their anger:

- Not eating
- Acting rebellious
- Not sleeping well
- Changing study habits
- Hanging out with new people
- Experimenting with new behavior, such as using tobacco, alcohol, and drugs

Many teens turn to alcohol and drugs when they want to express their anger. Instead of resorting to dangerous and habit-forming substances, there are healthier ways of working through anger.

Stage 3: Bargaining

Bargaining is another stage in the grieving process. Like most people, teens will do anything to avoid having their lives turned upside down and experiencing the pain of loss.

Jacob knew in his heart that his parents' divorce was the best outcome for everyone. Even so, before his mother had left, Jacob began to "bargain" with his parents to keep them together, as if by behaving in a certain way he could change the decision they had made. He began to do things that he thought would make his parents' life together less stressful. Jacob cleaned the house regularly, from top to bottom, without being asked to do so. He became more cooperative and responsible about looking after Max, and he did many special things for his parents. Through his actions, Jacob was trying to say, "If you stay together, I will help make things better around here." Unconsciously, he was asking himself, "What can I do to stop this?"

Younger children often think that their parents are divorcing because of them. Even though older children may know that the divorce has nothing to do with them, they may have some lingering feelings of guilt. "If I had been different, if I had been better," children sometimes feel, "my parents might still be together." Younger children promise to change their ways or "be good"; teens will try to intervene in other ways, as Jacob did.

Stage 4: Sadness

Sadness is a natural response to learning that your parents are splitting up. The underlying causes for your feelings are easy to

Sadness is a natural and entirely appropriate response to loss, particularly to the loss of your family as you know it. Understand that what you're feeling is OK and that you will stop being sad as time passes.

understand. For example, you recognize that your relationship with your parents will be different. You know that you will have to leave one parent to live with another. You feel sad for your parents, too, because you care about them and you know what they are going through makes them very sad. You know that your life will never be the same again, and that thought makes you very sad. It is important to be honest with yourself about these feelings. They are quite normal. If you do not face them, they will find a resting place somewhere within you and, sometime in the future, interfere with healthy emotional responses to other situations.

Stage 5: Fear

If you know that you have to go someplace that you have never been to before, and you have heard nothing but bad things about it, it is understandable that you might be afraid. It is much the same with learning that your parents are separating. In a way, the news means that you will be going somewhere that you have never been, and everyone has certainly heard a lot of negative things about life after divorce.

It is very common to fear the unknown, and fear of the unknown can be more terrifying than actually experiencing it. When you are able to face this feeling and tell others how you feel, you will find that it is not as difficult as you might have thought. You will learn that others have had similar feelings and experiences. You will learn how they managed to cope with those feelings. Fear is a normal and natural response during the early stages of a family's breakup. Your parents are scared, too. Sensing their fear can cause you to feel even more insecure.

Stage 6: Blame

When something bad happens, it is natural to look for an explanation. It is unsettling to think that things can just happen and that there is sometimes little or nothing that you can do about it. So you look for a reason and, sometimes, someone to blame.

If the divorce is sudden, the parent who leaves is the one who is usually blamed. In the case of longstanding arguments, complaints, and bickering, blame goes from one parent to the other on a regular basis. Children often see blame for the situation first expressed by their parents, whom they may have seen openly argue and blame each other.

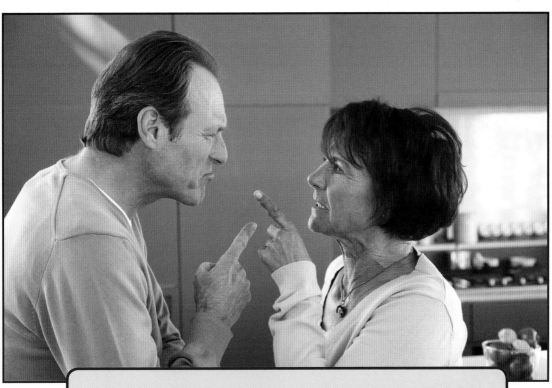

Trying to find the person to blame for your parents' divorce might make you feel better for a while. But divorce is rarely one person's fault, and blaming others or yourself can do damage.

Younger children often blame themselves for the divorce. Teens, even though they know that they did not cause the problem, sometimes blame themselves for not being able to stop it from happening. You might find yourself caught up in this blaming game. You might blame one parent or the other for not preventing it.

Stage 7: Acceptance

At last, if a teen is able to work through these feelings and stages, he or she will reach the stage of acceptance. At this point, teens have resigned themselves to the fact that their parents are splitting up. This is a positive goal because it means you can move on.

There is no definite time period for each of these stages. Some teens will stay in the denial stage longer than others will. Some may reach the acceptance stage before others. Some regress to stages they've already experienced. The point here is to understand that there is a normal process of getting through this very difficult period in your life.

CHAPTER THREE

WHEN YOU FEEL CAUGHT IN THE MIDDLE

Before your parents split up, you may have thought of them as a unit. Even though you knew they were separate people, you might never have thought of them as two distinct beings, each with their own personalities and goals. Maybe you were a little closer to one of them, but chances are you never imagined a day when you might have to choose between them.

After learning of her parents' divorce, Mya became withdrawn to the point that she found it impossible to take sides. The most she felt capable of was wishing that the whole thing would go away. She empathized with her mother's pain and disappointment, and she felt anger toward her father for his actions. Yet it was too painful for her to side with either parent.

So she became a passive bystander, which only made her feel more powerless and depressed. Although it seems

You may feel caught in the middle as your parents begin to start their separate lives. If they are making you feel the need to take sides, have a talk with them. Tell them it is important that you try to remain neutral.

normal and natural to identify with the parent who you think has been wronged, this is not such an easy thing to do; it is difficult to align yourself with one parent against the other. For Mya, siding with her mother would have meant siding against her father, and this was too difficult for her to do.

It can be difficult for children of divorcing parents to remain loyal to both parents. When your parents are together, you feel a sense of balance, togetherness, and unity. You have the sense that everyone feels the same way about each other. It is normal for teens who are aware of the circumstances leading to the divorce, whether they are sudden or long-term problems, to struggle with their feelings regarding the divorce or separation.

Children might side with the parent to whom they feel closer, or they might side with the parent they feel has been wronged in the process. Yet as children take sides, another conflict can develop in the form of guilt about favoring one parent over the other. When this happens, they may blame one or both parents for these feelings.

RESOLVING CONFLICT

Conflict is a part of life. Sometimes conflict can be resolved without much difficulty. Other times much effort will be required in order to reach a resolution. Some conflict will not be resolved. However, it is always advantageous to try to

(continued on next page)

(continued from previous page)

resolve conflict, and almost any attempt to resolve it is beneficial. Through these attempts, individuals can learn about themselves.

Unresolved conflict between people can lead to deeper problems and greater personal dissatisfaction in the long term. Some people attempt to ease these feelings through unhealthy means such as alcohol or other substance abuse and other types of self-destructive behavior.

Conflict resolution is a skill that can be learned. Many professionals teach conflict resolution. For couples that are divorcing, these individuals are often divorce mediators. Their role is to help settle conflicts that arise from the division of property or conflicts over custody issues. Marital counselors or therapists help couples to resolve conflicts within their relationship. Any lessons you learn about resolving conflict can be applied to your future relationships.

Custody Issues

In a divorce, there is another element of taking sides that often affects children. Unless the parents are able to reach an agreement themselves on all the elements of the divorce, outside professionals often become involved. These can include lawyers, judges, therapists, psychologists, social workers, and other mediators and health care professionals. Dealing with your feelings by yourself is difficult enough; being asked to share them with strangers and outsiders can be nearly impossible.

The most common situation wherein teens and other children have direct contact with such professionals is when their parents cannot agree over who will have custody of the children. Custody is often thought of as determining with which parent the child will live, but it is actually the legal responsibility for raising and providing for the child. If one parent is given custody, generally the other has visitation rights.

When divorcing parents cannot agree over who will have responsibility for taking care of their children, a judge in a court of law makes the decision for them. Custody is often the most contentious issue in a divorce case.

In deciding which parent is to be given custody, judges often try to determine what would be in the best interest of the child. However, in most states, there is no law that sets specific

Sometimes parents cannot agree on custody issues and must go to court. It is rare that children are asked to show loyalty to one parent or the other. Do not be concerned about having to choose sides.

standards that judges have to use in such cases. For many years, the presumption was that the mother was the best parent to be assigned the responsibility for raising the children, unless she had proven to be negligent or abusive. Under this assumption, the most important role of the father was as the economic supporter of the family. Thus, the most common outcome of custody disputes was that the mother would be assigned custody of the child and the father would be assigned to pay the mother a certain amount for the economic support of the child.

Although this is still the most common outcome, in the last two decades an increasing number of fathers have received custody. Joint custody, in which parents share the responsibilities, has also become much more common.

Do children have to take sides in a custody dispute? Emotionally, it is often difficult not to. However, it is rare that a child, especially a younger child, would be made to testify in court, in front of a judge, about which parent he or she would prefer to live with. What is more likely to happen is that a professional assigned by the court—usually a psychologist, therapist, or social worker—will interview the child about his or her home life and his or her feelings about the situation, then issue a report to the court. The judge may or may not make decision about custody based on the recommendations in such reports.

In such situations, children may feel less like they are taking sides than that they are being torn apart emotionally by love for and loyalty to both parents. In such situations, it is important that children find someone to help them deal with their emotions. Ideally, this should not be a professional appointed by a court or someone who is working on the behalf of one of their parents in the custody matter. What children need is someone whose only interest is what is best for them, which is not always what is best for the parents. How children can find adults who can help them in such situations will be discussed later.

When a Parent Leaves

After Jacob's mother had gotten settled with his grandparents she contacted him. She wanted him and Max to live with her. Jacob was sad, confused, and angry. A part of him felt that he should stay with his father because, in spite of the family's history, he felt close to him. It saddened him to think of his father living all alone. Even though he had rebelled against his parents, he realized he loved both of them and found it difficult to separate from either of them.

So what did he do? He tried to sort out his thinking about the choice that he had to make. He thought about the consequences and issues involved with leaving or staying. He felt that if he stayed, he could keep his friends, attend the same school, and perhaps have even more freedom than he had with his mother. On the other hand, he would miss his mom and Max. Going with his mom, of course, would keep the family together. However, he might risk endangering the relationship that he had with his father. He was afraid of hurting either parent, yet he was unable to discuss his feelings with any of the professionals the court had assigned to the case. Jacob ran away and remained in hiding among his friends for six weeks.

Sometimes when parents begin to have marital difficulties, the mother leaves first. This usually adds to the teen's stress

Traditionally, mothers were granted custody and fathers received visitation rights. This is because the mother was thought of as the caregiver. Today, however, many fathers are given custody.

over the family's breakup. Traditionally, the mother is the one who provides the glue that binds the family together. Legally, this is reflected in the presumption that, in most cases, the mother is the one who should have custody. However, certain circumstances dictate the hard choices that parents sometimes make.

More divorced fathers are beginning to raise children alone. Single mothers, too, can and do raise families successfully. As long as teens have a secure home headed by a responsible, supportive, and caring parent, they will most likely be assured of healthy development.

It is normal for children to want their parents to stay together. Perhaps Jacob's running away was his way of trying to let his parents know how he felt. It may also have been an attempt to delay, or stall, the process in the hope that they would stay together. He felt guilty because he believed the family was abandoning his father. Jacob's father had lost his job, and the family income had dwindled to half what it had been. Even though his mother told him she would be able to get a better job, he was nevertheless concerned about the family's situation, wondering whether or not they would be able to survive. These are common concerns that all children have when their parents are separating or divorcing.

Mya was devastated over the breakup of her family and suffering from the immediate shock of learning about it. Another aspect of her grief was her knowledge of the impact that her father's leaving would have on the family.

Mya's mother worked only part-time and earned very little money. Mya feared that the financial burden her mother would have to face would be overwhelming. Mya had little knowledge about child support or alimony. These financial questions caused her a great deal of fear and anxiety. She worried that their lives would change drastically and feared that her mother would be forced to get a full-time job. Her mother had been ill, and Mya thought that she would find it difficult to work full-time.

Mya wondered if they would have to move to a smaller place, or whether they would have to leave the area altogether. These are unknowns that are commonly felt during the early stages of the divorce process. During this stage, when your feelings are still very new and intense and you are not quite sure how to deal with them, it is important to talk over your thoughts and feelings with someone.

Divorce isn't limited to children with a mother and a father. Some children of same-sex marriages must also cope with divorce. These situations can be complicated by the fact that only one parent may be considered the legal parent of the child. In some cases, the parent who does not have any legal rights to the child moves on, ending his or her relationship with the child entirely.

Do Not Take Sides

It is uncomfortable to be in the middle of the emotions involved in your parents' separation. Adolescents choose a variety of ways to stay out of the middle. Some parents help their teens by shielding them from their own conflicts as much as possible.

For some parents, however, the process is more overwhelming, and their children inevitably are brought into the middle of it. Parents use various tactics to engage their teens in the conflict. Some parents unwittingly seek the help of their teens to support them in the conflict and sometimes use their children to gain information about the activities of the other spouse. These tactics can prove extremely detrimental to teens in the long run and make the early stage of the divorce or separation process even more difficult.

In emotional terms, Mya chose to get out of the middle by withdrawing totally. Although it is understandable, it is clear that in many ways this was not the best decision for her. She became disconnected from her parents and lost within herself. She was

It is not up to you to save your parents' marriage. Their marriage is their responsibility. The only ones who can solve the problems your parents are experiencing are your parents.

unable to resolve any of the inner conflicts that she felt or the conflicts involving the breakup of her family. She needed to find a way to remain connected to both parents but disconnected from their conflict.

Let Your Parents Work Out Their Own Problems

Sometimes adolescents take on the responsibility of trying to help their parents work things out. This, of course, produces more anxiety and stress and keeps you in the middle of the conflict. Why do parents divorce? There are probably as many different reasons as there are divorces. One thing is for certain, though: it is never the child's fault or the child's responsibility. Parents divorce or separate for their own reasons, and they must work through the conflict in their own way.

When the normal flow and structure of the family breaks down, adolescents often attempt to take on adult responsibilities. Although it is admirable to act as grown-up as possible about any situation, teens are not adults, and they should not expect themselves to resolve, handle, or deal with adult problems. Very few adults handle divorce well, so their children should not be surprised if they find themselves overwhelmed at times. The best thing to do is to admit that the situation can be overwhelming, then take it from there.

Jacob found himself squarely in the middle of his parents' problems. He wanted to help, as teens often do in such situations. When he found he could not fix the problem, he blamed himself rather than realizing that only his parents could solve their problems. In response, he withdrew and rebelled.

When he was a child, his parents' arguments had made him afraid. As a teenager, he felt anger and resentment. Yet a part of him felt that he could help. He got involved in the arguments, trying to understand why his parents were not able to get along. He would talk to his parents separately, but his efforts to mediate their conflict brought him too close to their disagreements. Ultimately, this only made their separation more difficult for him to accept. Jacob had to learn how to separate himself from his parents' conflicts.

CHAPTER FOUR

HOW TO ADAPT TO YOUR NEW LIFE

I t seems crazy to say, but divorce does not have to be an altogether bad thing. Of course, there's no denying that the experience is traumatic and challenging. However, once the initial shock and difficulty in adjusting pass, a loving family can emerge. It won't be the same as your old family, but that doesn't have to mean it will be worse. In fact, in some circumstances, divorce can result in stronger relationships and an overall happier family.

This does not happen automatically, of course. It requires understanding, acceptance of the new way of life that will emerge, and careful communication among family members. In some cases, this kind of communication is a skill that family members need to learn, both individually and together. In the best case, you will begin to understand some of the positive outcomes of the breakup. You will learn to see each of your parents in a very different light. Though you learned to view them for the most part as a team, you will get to know them as individuals. With some resolution to the difficulties that separated them, your parents

You may find yourself spending more time with each of your parents after a divorce. Although you might miss seeing them together, you have the opportunity to get to know them better on their own.

may have more energy and time to put into their relationships with you.

You can draw new meanings from your relationship with each parent. You will broaden your horizons through the expansion of friendships and associations. Your parents will maintain some of their old friendships while they form new ones. You will learn how to adjust to these changed relationships and increase your level of maturity. Your life may actually become more stable without some of the conflicts that were present in the earlier stages of divorce or separation, allowing you to see your present and future more clearly.

Your own personality will emerge. You will begin to feel like your old self again. You will find that part of you is different and

The experience of going through a divorce can bring siblings closer together. The painful and challenging adjustment allows siblings to form a tight bond that few others understand.

part of you is the same. It will seem as though you have traveled through a dark tunnel and met danger along the way, and now you are outside in the bright sunshine again, feeling fairly safe and secure. The past is a part of you, but you welcome the present and it is beginning to feel OK.

Immediately after his mother left them, Jacob was quite aware of the peace and quiet that had entered into his life. He and Max no longer winced at the loud, angry voices and words that left them sad and bitter at the same time. They stopped worrying that anything they did or said might get one of their parents angry and that the result would inevitably be a fight. They found a greater sense of inner peace and quiet.

Jacob decided that he wanted to remain with his father. But Max went to live with their mother. Since they lived so far away, the plan was that Jacob would see his mother and Max during the summer months and on special holidays like Thanksgiving and Christmas.

Jacob's adjustment to his new life was slow and somewhat rocky in the beginning, but with the help of others, it began to improve. Jacob began to be more open to the support that had been offered to him. His school counselor ran a support group for children whose parents had recently divorced, and Jacob found this group to be helpful. Fellow students led the group, so he was listening to voices of experience. Jacob found in the group an avenue to express his feelings to an accepting and understanding peer group. Jacob's father became more available to him and appeared to be happy and more content with his life. He was able to listen to Jacob and share some of his own feelings. Thus, Jacob saw his father as more human and became more accepting of him.

Jacob missed his mother and Max greatly, of course. His mother telephoned him often, and they wrote letters to each other frequently. They made plans for when they would see each other again and discussed other important issues in their lives. Although he missed the day-to-day contact, in some ways Jacob found it easier to communicate with his mother now. There was simply less tension in the air. Through this frequent communication, they learned about each other's lives and maintained the continuity of family ties.

As things settled down for him and his fears about the future eased a little bit, Jacob was able to resume positive relationships with friends and no longer felt compelled to act out in negative ways. He also found it easy to make new friends when he visited his mother and Max.

The Benefits of Counseling

Jacob and his family did not work out this friendly state of affairs entirely on their own. In time the family was able to realize the benefit of the professional help they had received from counselors and therapists. They worked at incorporating into their new lives what they had learned about themselves and what they wanted for their future. The result was a fairly positive adjustment for the entire family after a long, bitter marital relationship.

With professional help, Mya, too, was able to move on. Probably because of the sudden nature of the separation and later divorce, Mya, Brielle, and their mother had a more difficult time healing. The girls received individual counseling and family counseling with their mother. Family counseling sometimes involved their father. With help and time they were able to restore

Counseling can be a tremendous benefit for families going through divorce. Under the guidance of a trained professional, each family member has the chance to express his or her feelings, fears, and hopes for the future.

the loving relationship they had shared with their parents before the problems began.

Individual counseling helped Mya to get over her depression. She began to have a better understanding of how to cope with her circumstances. She learned that it was OK to love both her parents. The anger that she felt toward her father began to diminish.

In her own counseling, Mya's sister, Brielle, was able to talk about her feelings concerning what was happening to her family. She developed a better understanding of why she had suddenly become so driven and why she seemed to have such a need to keep moving. She settled back into a normal pace. Noise in the form of disruption, negative feelings, sudden hostility, and anger subsided. The family members found a new way of relating to each other.

Open and Honest Communication

Both families learned that communicating openly and honestly was the key to calming their fears and easing the burdens of their changing lifestyle. Through honest communication, the teens came to better understand some of the reasons why their parents chose to separate.

Until they were able to talk to each other about what was happening to them, the teens could only question and guess about what was going to happen to them, and the questioning and guessing caused inner conflict and confusion. Communication opened doors to improved understanding of how they would live their lives apart from a parent or siblings. This opening up helped the parents, as well, to develop a better vision for their future. Teens need to know that their parents love them and want to continue to guide them and make life as good as it can be. Hearing this directly from their parents reassures them and gives them comfort and confidence in their future.

Major Adjustments

Adjusting to your life will have its high moments and its low moments. You may have to adjust to many new things: a new relationship with your parents, a new home, new friends, and a new community, for instance. You may be saying good-bye to old friends and having to find new ways to maintain those friendships. You will also be learning to adjust to new relationships in

After the shock, anger, and sadness subside, you will have a chance to develop a strong new relationship with each parent. The key is to find a way to communicate honestly about how you are feeling.

your parents' lives. The latter is probably one of the most difficult adjustments of all. Even though your parents' custody arrangement will separate you physically from one of your parents, the separation does not necessarily have to interfere with the parental influence that your parent had and will continue to have in your development. That parent might, in fact, become an even stronger influence in your life. You and your parent may learn to place an even greater value on the time you have together.

It may take added effort on the part of your absent parent and you to develop and maintain this closeness, but the effort is worth it. When this happens, you will begin to seek advice of the absent parent in positive ways. Keep in mind that some teens use the absent parent to challenge the advice or directions of the custodial parent. This is a negative way to respond to your situation and can prolong the adjustment period.

CHAPTER FIVE

LIVING YOUR NEW LIFE

After your parents split up, you will find yourself living a different life. Since you most likely will be living with a single parent, chances are you'll be left alone more than you were. You might be entrusted to new and greater responsibilities, like caring for your younger sibling or starting dinner preparations. Adapting to this new life will be challenging, but it will allow you to develop important life skills that will serve you well in the future.

Embrace Your New Home

Your parents' divorce may mean that you have to move away from your area. This change in your life will have an impact on your friendships. When divorce necessitates a move to another town or city, it means that you will be saying good-bye to old friends. However, this does not mean that you have to say good-bye to the friendships. You can still see each other on your visits back home with the other parent, and you will find ways to communicate through letters, e-mail, telephone, video chats, or social

Moving out of your childhood home is a big change in an already confusing time. Keep an open mind, and embrace the idea that you have a chance to start fresh in a new place, where you can make new memories.

media. If your friendship is important to the two of you, you will both find a way to maintain it by keeping up with the news about what is going on in each other's worlds.

When Your Parents Find New Love

Adjusting to a one-parent family is a challenge in itself, but you may also be faced with an even bigger challenge, which is becoming accustomed to your parents dating new people.

Dating and remarriage is probably as prevalent as divorce. Most couples do remarry after divorce. If your parents start to see other people, or perhaps even decide to remarry, you will face many different emotional challenges. First and foremost, it may be a challenge to stay out of the middle of the developing relationship.

It is natural to look for comparisons between this new individual and your parent. On the other hand, liking this person too much might place you in that uncomfortable middle position again. One parent might question his or her child about the activities of the other parent. This places more of a burden on you as you struggle with this new life, but in time, you will learn to adjust to these new relationships.

The challenge to any relationship is how to deal with the inevitable changes that occur. Many things affect people: work, personal issues, financial issues, and family issues. Adults are constantly confronted with these challenges. Sometimes they become overwhelming and begin to cause stress in family relations.

Divorce usually begins with some kind of conflict. Regardless of how the conflict starts, some parents find it difficult to find a resolution to it. Parents may seek family or couples counseling. When they choose this route, some get the help they need either to go their separate ways or to remain in the marriage with a better understanding between them.

Important lessons can be learned from divorce. Teens can learn about conflict and how to resolve it. They can learn how to maintain relationships through love, caring, and support of one another. They learn about forgiveness. Teens learn that life goes on. They learn that even if their parents are with other people, their parents' love for them will continue. Teens will find that they can adjust to the new people in their parents' lives.

Your parent might find love with a new person. That could mean making room in your life for stepsiblings or half siblings. This is a challenge, for sure, but it is also an opportunity to gain an incredible family.

Divorce can teach teens about attachments and the true meaning of family. When a family separates, it is important that the parents continue to be involved in their children's lives. If parents continue to maintain family ties, teens cannot only survive the divorce but thrive, in the process learning valuable lessons about what things are really important in life.

Use What You've Learned

Teens who have experienced the separation or divorce of their parents often show increased maturity in many ways. This

HOW TO RESOLVE CONFLICTS

People find many ways to resolve conflict. There are simple steps that can be followed, however, that lend assistance to this process. The first step is laying the cards on the table.

In this stage, each party to the conflict presents his or her view of the situation. The key is that each party agrees to listen to the other's point of view about the problem without interruption. What you are trying to do is understand the other party's thinking while giving him or her the chance to understand your own. This step is preparation for reaching an agreement.

The next step is finding common ground. In this stage you are trying to find some point, no matter how small, that the two of you can agree on. The two parties have to agree to accept some degree of mutual responsibility for the conflict or problem and look for areas of compromise.

The third step is commitment. After both parties have laid their cards on the table and found some common ground, you are then ready to look for points of agreement between the two of you that will lead to commitment. Hopefully, after these steps are taken, you will be able to commit to taking actions that will resolve the disagreement or dispute and prevent future occurrences.

maturity may stem from discovering that family security, stability, and happiness are not guarantees and should never be taken for granted. They have also discovered that love, by itself, is not always enough to ward off disagreement and conflict.

They watched as their parents struggled with themselves and with each other in their attempts to smooth the wrinkles in

You can take everything you learned through experiencing your parents' divorce and turn it into a positive for yourself. Going through massive changes and learning to resolve conflict will help you in future relationships.

their lives. As their parents formed new relationships, they had to experience adjustments that other teens did not experience. Teen children of divorced parents must adjust not only to changes in their relationships with their parents but also to the changes in their own friendships. Teens learn that you can adjust to these changes. Finally, they learn the important lesson of forgiveness.

Through experiencing the changing nature of relationships, teens learn valuable lessons about what to expect when they are confronted with conflict or choice in their own relationships.

When people are confronted with individual differences or inner conflicts, there is not always an easy answer. Teens also learn how to adapt to the changes in their own friendships. Even though Jacob stayed in his old home when his mother and brother moved away, he was changed in some way by his circumstances. As he changed, so did his interactions with his friends. Do not be surprised if after your parents' divorce, you begin to see yourself differently. This means that you have learned something about yourself.

Spending more time with his father afforded Jacob the opportunity to see his father in a different light. He came to understand the importance of cooperation. He and his father began to take the time to talk to each other about their feelings. Jacob no longer felt the need to seek a family among his friends, and the nature of his friendships changed. He found himself in greater control of his actions.

The Gift of Forgiveness

Another important lesson is forgiveness. Jacob and Mya observed that in time their parents forgave each other. Forgiveness is important because it allows you to get rid of anger. Anger is a very destructive emotion, which causes individuals to make poor, regrettable choices. It is quite enough to witness or be involved in an environment filled with stress and conflict. Holding on to anger and resentment only prolongs these feelings and prevents the healing from taking place.

In time, Mya's mother was able to forgive her husband for the choice that he made. Though it took a long time, she was able to do it. Mya and her sister benefited by this example of forgiveness.

In time, you might see that your family is able to exist happily. It won't be the same as it was. However, by treating each other with forgiveness and respect, your new family might be stronger. And you definitely will be.

Mya began to see her mother differently. At first she saw her mother as weak and less capable. She was angry with her mother for being this way. Mya was also angry with her father because she felt that he took advantage of her mother. This inner turmoil caused her to dislike both of her parents. Once she saw that her parents were able to forgive each other, she was able to forgive each of them.

While no one wants their parents to divorce, it doesn't have to ruin your life if they do. Hopefully, this resource has given you some ideas about why parents sometimes decide to split up. You also have learned how to prepare for the feelings you will experience and to cope with the many changes that are coming your way. Most important, you should focus on what you can gain from a terrible situation. Even though a divorce is life-changing, you can still have a positive and loving relationship with both your parents. Though there is no denying that divorce represents an end to certain things in your life, it can be the beginning of positive new things as well.

GLOSSARY

ACTING OUT Responding to unresolved stress or inner conflict by behaving in harmful, destructive, or uncharacteristic ways.

ALIMONY Court-ordered provision for one spouse to provide financial support to the other.

BARGAINING One of the stages of grief, in which a person desperately looks for ways to avoid the loss or bad thing that has happened.

CHILD SUPPORT Court-ordered, legally obligated payments made by a noncustodial parent that contribute to the financial care of raising his or her child.

COMMON GROUND A foundation of common interest that allows for mutual understanding.

CONFLICT RESOLUTION Process of finding solutions to a dispute that minimize the destructive consequences of the disagreement and are mutually satisfactory to both parties.

CONTENTIOUS Causing an argument or conflict.

CUSTODY Literally, immediate supervision and control. In the context of divorce, custody refers to which parent is assigned the legal responsibility for raising the children of the marriage.

DENIAL In psychology, a defense mechanism whereby a person deals with a situation that is causing stress or conflict by denying the existence or reality of the situation.

DEPRESSION Psychological condition characterized by prolonged feelings of sadness, hopelessness, worthlessness, or despair.

DIVORCE The legal termination of a marriage.

GRIEF Long-lasting or deep distress, most often caused by a death or profound loss.

JOINT CUSTODY Legal decision that both parents will share custody of their child or children.

MARRIAGE The legal and/or religious union of a man and woman as husband and wife.

MEDIATOR A person who works with two sides—whether it's a divorcing couple or two organizations—to help them resolve their conflict.

NEGLIGENT Failing to take proper care of someone or something.

PHYSIOLOGICAL Pertaining to the healthy or normal functioning of an organism.

PROFOUND Great or intense.

SURROGATE Substitute.

THERAPIST A person trained in methods of treatment and rehabilitation other than the use of drugs or surgery, especially in treatment of emotional or psychological issues.

FOR MORE INFORMATION

Al-Anon Family Group Headquarters, Inc.
1600 Corporate Landing Parkway
Virginia Beach, VA 23454
(757) 563-1600
Website: http://www.al-anon.org
This site can link you to local Al-Anon meetings—a great place
   to go for help if you live with an alcoholic parent or
   stepparent.

American Association for Marriage and Family Therapy
112 South Alfred Street
Alexandria, VA 22314-3061
(703) 838-9808
Website: http://www.aamft.org
This organization offers support and suggestions for seeking
   family therapy to cope with divorce and blended families.

Childhelp USA Hotline
(800) 422-4453
This hotline is available in English and Spanish for young people
   in crisis.

Children's Defense Fund (CDF)
25 E Street NW
Washington, DC 20001
(800) 233-1200
Website: http://www.childrensdefense.org
CDF provides a voice for all the children of America who cannot
   vote, lobby, or speak for themselves. CDF educates the
   nation about the needs of children and encourages

preventive investments before they get sick, drop out of school, get into trouble, or suffer family breakdown.

Children's Rights Council
1296 Cronson Boulevard, Suite 3086
Crofton, MD 21114
(301) 459-1220
Website: http://www.crckids.org
The Children's Rights Council is dedicated to helping divorced, separated, and never married parents remain actively and responsibly involved in their child's life. Parents can join local groups to help them deal with their situation.

Stepfamily Foundation
310 West 85th Street, Suite 1B
New York, NY 10024
(212) 877-3244
Website: http://www.stepfamily.org
This nonprofit organization provides counseling for the step-family or blended family, divorce counseling, remarriage counseling, and stepfamily certification seminars.

Websites

Because of the changing nature of Internet links, Rosen Publishing has developed an online list of websites related to the subject of this book. This site is updated regularly. Please use this link to access this list:

http://www.rosenlinks.com/DIV/unders

FOR FURTHER READING

Baker, Amy J. L., and Katherine Andre. *Getting Through My Parents' Divorce*. Oakland, CA: Instant Help Books, 2015.

Bergin, Rory M., and Jared Meyer. *Frequently Asked Questions About Divorce*. New York, NY: Rosen Publishing, 2012.

Bryfonski, Dedria. *Child Custody*. Farmington Hills, MI: Greenhaven Press, 2011.

Espejo, Roman. *Custody and Divorce*. Detroit, MI: Greenhaven Press, 2013.

Gay, Kathlyn. *Divorce: The Ultimate Teen Guide*. Lanham, MD: Rowman & Littlefield, 2014.

Iorizzo, Carrie. *Divorce and Blended Families*. St. Catharines, Ontario: Crabtree Publishing Company, 2013.

Kavanaugh, Dorothy. *Hassled Girl?: Girls Dealing with Feelings*. Berkeley Heights, NJ: Enslow Publishers, 2014.

McLaughlin, Jerry, and Katherine E. Krohn. *Dealing with Your Parents' Divorce*. New York, NY: Rosen Publishing, 2016.

Peterman, Rosie L., Jared Meyer, and Charlie Quill. *Divorce and Stepfamilies*. New York, NY: Rosen Publishing, 2013.

Stewart, Sheila, and Rae Simons. *I Live in Two Homes: Adjusting to Divorce and Remarriage*. Broomall, PA: Mason Crest Publishers, 2011.

INDEX

statistics on divorce, 6
stepfamily, 6
substance abuse, 6, 28

T

taking sides, 25–27, 28, 30, 34
teenage years, changes that
    occur during, 10–11, 12
therapy, 27, 28, 30, 42–44, 49
tobacco use, 19

V

victim, feeling like a, 18–19

W

withdrawal, 18, 25, 34, 36

About the Authors

Becky Lenarki was employed as a social worker for thirty years. She enjoys spending time with her grandchildren, who are part of a happily blended family.

Florence Calhoun is a writer and counselor in Virginia.

Photo Credits